I
HAVE

By

L. O. Ovbije

ISBN: 978-1-944411-15-2
Copyright © 2023 by Rev. L O. Ovbije
Ovbije World Outreach Ministries, Inc.
P.O. Box 966
Clarkston, GA 30021-0966

Website: owom.org
Email: theword@owom.org

Published by SOIL Foundation, Inc.
P.O. Box 966
Clarkston, GA 30021-0966

DEDICATION

To God the Father, who love the world he created and sent into the world Jesus Christ his only begotten Son, To Jesus Christ who came into this world in the flesh, died, buried and rose from the dead triumphantly, to redeem every human being God created and God made in his own image and likeness, this Jesus Christ of Nazareth has made redemption available for any human being that will trust and believe in him. And to the Holy Spirit, who continuously reveal Jesus Christ to individuals and people daily.

I thank God for my dear father who taught me discipline and my precious mother who taught me grace and forgiveness. Both taught me unconditional love. Both love me unconditionally. I love both of them dearly and unconditionally. Pray in the language you speak daily. Do not pray to impress people or God. There is no language on earth that is superior to your own language. Pray in your own language. Pray in the language you understand, God wants to hear from you now.

I Timothy 3:16

ACKNOWLEDGMENTS

To my wonderful parents: Chief J. E. Ovbije & Mrs. Margaret O. Ovbije, and to my siblings. My father was a man that lived a life that left an excellent and lasting impression on me. My father and mother taught me unconditional love; my mother taught me grace and forgiveness. Our family knew the meaning of a loving, secure and rich home because of my father's presence. I thank God for the private elementary school at Sapele: Children Nursery School, where I attended. It was there that I encounter God for the first time in prayer in a very early age.

To my precious pastor and his lovely wife, both were strong examples of a man and a woman devoted to God. I was fortunate to have pastor & Mrs. Umukoro, both disciples me. I thank them both for their daily early Morning Prayer life. To the men of God who also impacted my prayer life, W. F. Kumuyi and Benjamin Udi.

Finally to my sweet, precious, wonderful wife: Theresa Spearman Ovbije, a woman of God, whom I simply call "sweetie".

PREFACE

God is who he says he is:
Behold, I am the LORD, the God of all
flesh: is there any thing too hard for me?
Jeremiah 32:27

I am who God says I am:
But ye are a chosen generation, a royal
priesthood, an holy nation, a peculiar
people; that ye should shew forth the
praises of him who hath called you out of
darkness into his marvellous light;
1 Peter 2:9

God has what he says he has:
The earth is the LORD's, and the fulness
thereof; the world, and they that dwell
therein.
Psalm 24:1

I have what God says I have:
According as his divine power hath given
unto us all things that pertain unto life
and godliness, through the knowledge of
him that hath called us to glory and

virtue:
2 Peter 1:3

God will do what he says he will do:
God is not a man, that he should lie;
neither the son of man, that he should
repent: hath he said, and shall he not do
it? or hath he spoken, and shall he not
make it good?
Numbers 23:19

I can do what God says I can do:
I can do all things through Christ which
strengtheneth me.
Philippians 4:13

I am forever grateful to God and my
parents, for my parents instilled in me
from infant age who I am and whom I
am. Both of my parents never spoke
negative of me or about me. They believe
the best of me. They always encourage
me. They spoke great creative words into
my life. They believe and say to me again
and again, over and over, that I can
succeed in any good thing I put my heart
to do. They are my forever champions.

A

I Have Authority:

Then he called his twelve disciples together, and gave them power and authority over all devils, and to cure diseases. St. Luke 9:1

I Have Abundance:

Now unto him that is able to do exceeding abundantly above all that we ask or think, according to the power that worketh in us, Ephesians 3:20

I Have An Angel:

Are they not all ministering spirits, sent forth to minister for them who shall be heirs of

salvation?
Hebrews 1:14

I Have An Access To God:

Let us therefore come boldly unto the throne of grace, that we may obtain mercy, and find grace to help in time of need.
Hebrews 4:16

I Have An Anointing:

But the anointing which ye have received of him abideth in you, and ye need not that any man teach you: but as the same anointing teacheth you of all things, and is truth, and is no lie, and even as it hath taught you, ye shall abide in him.
1 John 2:27

B

I Have Boldness:

In whom we have boldness and access with confidence by the faith of him.
Ephesians 3:12

I Have The Blood Of Jesus:

After the same manner also he took the cup, when he had supped, saying, this cup is the new testament in my blood: this do ye, as oft as ye drink it, in remembrance of me.
1 Corinthians 11:25

I Have A Buckler:

The Lord is my rock, and my fortress, and my deliverer; my

God, my strength, in whom I will trust; my buckler, and the horn of my salvation, and my high tower.
Psalm 18:2

I Have A Blessing:

Blessed be the God and Father of our Lord Jesus Christ, who hath blessed us with all spiritual blessings in heavenly places in Christ:
Ephesians 1:3

I Have The Bread Life:

This is the bread which cometh down from heaven, that a man may eat thereof, and not die.
St. John 6:50

C

I Have Christ.

To whom God would make known what is the riches of the glory of this mystery among the Gentiles; which is Christ in you, the hope of glory:
Colossians 1:27

I Have A Comforter:

And I will pray the Father, and he shall give you another Comforter, that he may abide with you for ever;
St. John 14:16

I Have A Captain:

For it became him, for whom are all things, and by whom are

all things, in bringing many sons
unto glory, to make
the captain of their salvation
perfect through sufferings.
Hebrews 2:10

I Have A Calling:

Wherefore the rather, brethren,
give diligence to make your
calling and election sure: for if
ye do these things, ye shall never
fall:
2 Peter 1:10

I Have Confidence:

For the LORD shall be thy
confidence, and shall keep thy
foot from being taken.
Proverbs 3:26

D

I Have A Defender:

Yea, the Almighty shall be thy defence, and thou shalt have plenty of silver.
Job 22:25

I Have Direction:

Thy word is a lamp unto my feet, and a light unto my path.
Psalms 119:105

I Have Dominion:

And God said, Let us make man in our image, after our likeness: and let them have dominion over the fish of the sea, and over the fowl of the air, and over the cattle, and over all the earth,

and over every creeping thing
that creepeth upon the earth.
Genesis 1:26

I Have A Deliverer:

The Lord is my rock, and my
fortress, and my deliverer; my
God, my strength, in whom I
will trust; my buckler, and the
horn of my salvation, and my
high tower.
Psalm 18:2

E

I Have Eternal Life:

That whosoever believeth in him should not perish, but have eternal life.
St. John 3:15

I Have Excellent Spirit:

Forasmuch as an excellent spirit, and knowledge, and understanding, interpreting of dreams, and shewing of hard sentences, and dissolving of doubts, were found in the same Daniel, whom the king named Belteshazzar: now let Daniel be called, and he will shew the interpretation.
Daniel 5:12

I Have An Expectation:

So shall the knowledge of wisdom be unto thy soul: when thou hast found it, then there shall be a reward, and thy expectation shall not be cut off. Proverbs 24:14

I Have An Experience:

And patience, experience; and experience, hope: Romans 5:4

I Have Eyes Which See:

And he turned him unto his disciples, and said privately, Blessed are the eyes which see the things that ye see: St. Luke 10:23

<u>F</u>

I Have Faith:

Wherefore I also, after I heard of your faith in the Lord Jesus, and love unto all the saints, Ephesians 1:15

I Have Forgiveness:

In whom we have redemption through his blood, even the forgiveness of sins: Colossians 1:14

I Have Fellowship:

That which we have seen and heard declare we unto you, that ye also may have fellowship with us: and truly our fellowship is with the Father, and with his

Son Jesus Christ.
1 John 1:3

I Have Favour:

So shalt thou find favour and
good understanding in the sight
of God and man.
Proverbs 3:4

I Have A Father:

Now unto God and our Father
be glory for ever and ever.
Amen.
Philippians 4:20

I Have Fruits:

The husbandman that laboureth
must be first partaker of the
fruits.
2 Timothy 1:6

G

I Have The Guide:

Howbeit when he, the Spirit of truth, is come, he will guide you into all truth: for he shall not speak of himself; but whatsoever he shall hear, that shall he speak: and he will shew you things to come.
St. John 16:13

I Have Grace:

But unto every one of us is given grace according to the measure of the gift of Christ.
Ephesians 4:7

I Have Glory:

And the glory which thou gavest me I have given them; that they may be one, even as we are one: St. John 17:22

I Have A Gift:

For the gifts and calling of God are without repentance.
Romans 11:29

I Have A Good Name:

A good name is rather to be chosen than great riches, and loving favour rather than silver and gold.
Proverbs 22:1

<u>H</u>

I Have The Holy Ghost:

He said unto them, Have ye
received the Holy Ghost since ye
believed? And they said unto
him, We have not so much as
heard whether there be any
Holy Ghost.
Acts 19:2

I Have A High Priest:

Wherefore, holy brethren,
partakers of the heavenly
calling, consider the Apostle and
High Priest of our profession,
Christ Jesus;
Hebrews 3:1

I Have Hope:

Now faith is the substance of things hoped for, the evidence of things not seen.
Hebrews 11:1

I Have An Helper:

Behold, God is mine helper: the Lord is with them that uphold my soul.
Psalm 54:4

I Have A Heart:

Speaking to yourselves in psalms and hymns and spiritual songs, singing and making melody in your heart to the Lord;
Ephesians 5:19

I

I Have An Inheritance:

In whom also we have obtained an inheritance, being predestinated according to the purpose of him who worketh all things after the counsel of his own will:
Ephesians 1:11

I Have An Invitation:

Let us therefore come boldly unto the throne of grace, that we may obtain mercy, and find grace to help in time of need.
Hebrews 4:16

I Have An Intercessor:

Wherefore he is able also to save them to the uttermost that come unto God by him, seeing he ever liveth to make intercession for them.
Hebrews 7:25

I Have An Integrity:

The just man walketh in his integrity: his children are blessed after him.
Proverbs 20:7

I Have An Inner Witness:

The Spirit itself beareth witness with our spirit, that we are the children of God:
Romans 8:16

J

I Have Fullness of Joy:

These things have I spoken unto you, that my joy might remain in you, and that your joy might be full.
St. John 15:11

I Have The Joy Of The Lord:

Then he said unto them, Go your way, eat the fat, and drink the sweet, and send portions unto them for whom nothing is prepared: for this day is holy unto our Lord: neither be ye sorry; for the joy of the Lord is your strength.
Nehemiah 8:10

I Have A Justifier:

To declare, I say, at this time his righteousness: that he might be just, and the justifier of him which believeth in Jesus.
Romans 3:26

I Have A Judge:

For the LORD is our judge, the LORD is our lawgiver, the LORD is our king; he will save us.
Isaiah 33:22

K

I Have Knowledge:

That in every thing ye are enriched by him, in all utterance, and in all knowledge;
1 Corinthians 1:5

I Have Kindness:

The desire of a man is his kindness: and a poor man is better than a liar.
Proverbs 19:22

I Have The Keys:

And I will give unto thee the keys of the kingdom of heaven: and whatsoever thou shalt bind on earth shall be bound in heaven: and

whatsoever thou shalt loose on
earth shall be loosed in heaven.
St. Matthew 16:19

I Have Knees:

O come, let us worship and bow
down: let us kneel before the
LORD our maker.
Psalm 95:6

I Have A Keeper:

The LORD is thy keeper: the
LORD is thy shade upon thy
right hand.
Psalm 121:5

L

I Have Love:

And hope maketh not ashamed; because the love of God is shed abroad in our hearts by the Holy Ghost which is given unto us.
Romans 5:5

I Have Life:

He that hath the Son hath <u>life</u>; and he that hath not the Son of God hath not life.
1 John 5:12

I Have Liberty:

And that because of false brethren unawares brought in, who came in privily to spy out

our liberty which we have in Christ Jesus, that they might bring us into bondage:
Galatians 2:4

I Have Light:

Let your light so shine before men, that they may see your good works, and glorify your Father which is in heaven.
St. Matthew 5:16

I Have A Lifter:

But thou, O LORD, art a shield for me; my glory, and the lifter up of mine head.
Psalm 3:3

<u>M</u>

I Have A Ministry:

And all things are of God, who hath reconciled us to himself by Jesus Christ, and hath given to us the ministry of reconciliation; 2 Corinthians 5:18

I Have Mercy:

Let us therefore come boldly unto the throne of grace, that we may obtain mercy, and find grace to help in time of need. Hebrews 4:16

I have Money:

Yea, the Almighty shall be thy defence, and thou shalt have

plenty of silver.
Job 22:25

I Have The Mind Of Christ:

For who hath known the mind of the Lord, that he may instruct him? but we have the mind of Christ.
1 Corinthians 2:16

I Have A Master:

The disciple is not above his master, nor the servant above his lord.
St. Matthew 10:24

N

I Have The Name Of Jesus:

And these signs shall follow them that believe; In my name shall they cast out devils; they shall speak with new tongues; St. Mark 16:17

I Have A New Commandment:

A new commandment I give unto you, That ye love one another; as I have loved you, that ye also love one another. St. John 13:34

I Have A New Heart:

A new heart also will I give you, and a new spirit will I put within you: and I will take away the

stony heart out of your flesh,
and I will give you an heart of
flesh.
Ezekiel 36:26

I Have A New Song:

And he hath put a new song in
my mouth, even praise unto our
God: many shall see it, and fear,
and shall trust in the LORD.
Psalm 40:3

I Have A New Spirit:

And I will give them one heart,
and I will put a new spirit within
you; and I will take the stony
heart out of their flesh, and will
give them an heart of flesh:
Ezekiel 11:19

O

I Have An Open Hand

For the poor shall never cease out of the land: therefore I command thee, saying, Thou shalt open thine hand wide unto thy brother, to thy poor, and to thy needy, in thy land.
Deuteronomy 15:11

I Have Obedience:

For your obedience is come abroad unto all men. I am glad therefore on your behalf: but yet I would have you wise unto that which is good, and simple concerning evil.
Romans 16:19

I Have An Offering:

Give unto the LORD the glory due unto his name: bring an offering, and come into his courts.
Psalm 96:8

I Have Opinion To Follow God:

And Elijah came unto all the people, and said, How long halt ye between two opinions? if the LORD be God, follow him: but if Baal, then follow him. And the people answered him not a word.
1 Kings 18:21

P

I Have Power:

Behold, I give unto you power to tread on serpents and scorpions, and over all the power of the enemy: and nothing shall by any means hurt you.
St. Luke 10:19

I Have Promises

Whereby are given unto us exceeding great and precious promises: that by these ye might be partakers of the divine nature, having escaped the corruption that is in the world through lust.
2 Peter 1:4

I Have Peace

Peace I leave with you, my peace
I give unto you: not as the world
giveth, give I unto you. Let not
your heart be troubled, neither
let it be afraid.
St. John 14:27

I Have Patience:

And to knowledge temperance;
and to temperance patience; and
to patience godliness;
2 Peter 1:6

I Have Prosperity:

Save now, I beseech thee,
O LORD: O LORD, I beseech
thee, send now prosperity.
Psalm 118:25

Q

I Have Quietness:

Better is a dry morsel, and quietness therewith, than an house full of sacrifices with strife.
Proverbs 17:1

I Have Quality Of Life:

The thief cometh not, but for to steal, and to kill, and to destroy: I am come that they might have life, and that they might have it more abundantly.
St. John 10:10

I Have

R

I Have Righteousness:

**But of him are ye in Christ Jesus, who of God is made unto us wisdom, and righteousness, and sanctification, and redemption:
1 Corinthians 1:30**

I Have Redemption:

**In whom we have redemption through his blood, the forgiveness of sins, according to the riches of his grace;
Ephesians 1:7**

I Have Received Christ:

As ye have therefore received Christ Jesus the Lord, so walk

ye in him:
Colossians 2:6

I Have Riches:

Wealth and riches shall be in his house: and his righteousness endureth for ever.
Psalms 112:3

I Have Revelation:

That the God of our Lord Jesus Christ, the Father of glory, may give unto you the spirit of wisdom and revelation in the knowledge of him:
Ephesians 1:17

S

I Have A Sound Mind:

For God hath not given us the spirit of fear; but of power, and of love, and of a sound mind.
2 Timothy 1:7

I Have Good Success:

This book of the law shall not depart out of thy mouth; but thou shalt meditate therein day and night, that thou mayest observe to do according to all that is written therein: for then thou shalt make thy
way prosperous, and then thou shalt have good success.
Joshua 1:8

I Have A Shepherd

The Lord is my shepherd; I
shall not want.
Psalm 23:1

I Have Seed To Sow:

Now he that ministereth seed to
the sower both minister bread
for your food, and multiply your
seed sown, and increase the
fruits of your righteousness;)
2 Corithians 9:10

I Have Sweet Sleep:

When thou liest down, thou
shalt not be afraid: yea, thou
shalt lie down, and thy sleep
shall be sweet.
Proverbs 3:24

T

I Have All Things:

According as his divine power hath given unto us all things that pertain unto life and godliness, through the knowledge of him that hath called us to glory and virtue:
2 Peter 1:3

I Have The Teacher:

But the Comforter, which is the Holy Ghost, whom the Father will send in my name, he shall teach you all things, and bring all things to your remembrance, whatsoever I have said unto you.
St. John 14:26

I Have Temperance:

And to knowledge temperance; and to temperance patience; and to patience godliness;
2 Peter 1:6

I Have An High Tower:

The Lord is my rock, and my fortress, and my deliverer; my God, my strength, in whom I will trust; my buckler, and the horn of my salvation, and my high tower.
Psalm 18:2

U

I Have Utterance:

That in every thing ye are enriched by him, in all utterance, and in all knowledge;
1 Corinthians 1:5

I Have Understanding:

The eyes of your understanding being enlightened; that ye may know what is the hope of his calling, and what the riches of the glory of his inheritance in the saints,
Ephesians 1:18

I Have An Unction:

But ye have an unction from the Holy One, and ye know all

things.
1 John 2:20

I Have Uprightness:

I know also, my God, that thou triest the heart, and hast pleasure in uprightness. As for me, in the uprightness of mine heart I have willingly offered all these things: and now have I seen with joy thy people, which are present here, to offer willingly unto thee.
1 Chronicles 29:17

V

I Have Virtue:

And beside this, giving all
diligence, add to your faith
virtue; and to virtue knowledge;
2 Peter 1:5

I Have The Victory:

The Lord shall cause thine
enemies that rise up against thee
to be smitten before thy face:
they shall come out against thee
one way, and flee before thee
seven ways.
Deuteronomy 28:7

I Have A Vessel:

But we have this treasure in
earthen vessels, that the

excellency of the power may be of God, and not of us.
2 Corinthians 4:7

I Have A Vision:

For the vision is yet for an appointed time, but at the end it shall speak, and not lie: though it tarry, wait for it; because it will surely come, it will not tarry.
Habakkuk 2:3

I Have Vocation:

I therefore, the prisoner of the Lord, beseech you that ye walk worthy of the vocation wherewith ye are called,
Ephesians 4:1

W

I Have Wisdom:

But of him are ye in Christ Jesus, who of God is made unto us wisdom, and righteousness, and sanctification, and redemption:
1 Corinthians 1:30

I Have A Witness:

The Spirit itself beareth witness with our spirit, that we are the children of God:
Romans 8:16

I Have The Word:

Thy word have I hid in mine heart, that I might not sin

against thee.
Psalms 119:11

I Have Wealth:

But thou shalt remember
the Lord thy God: for it is he
that giveth thee power to get
wealth, that he may establish his
covenant which he sware unto
thy fathers, as it is this day.
Deuteronomy 8:18

I Have A Weapon:

(For the weapons of our
warfare are not carnal, but
mighty through God to the
pulling down of strong holds;)
2 Corinthians 10:4

Y

I Have A Yield Fruits:

And other fell on good ground, and did yield fruit that sprang up and increased; and brought forth, some thirty, and some sixty, and some an hundred.
St. Mark 4:8

I Have Land Increasing Yield:

Yea, the LORD shall give that which is good; and our land shall yield her increase.
Psalm 85:12

I Have Yielding Peace:

Now no chastening for the present seemeth to be joyous, but grievous: nevertheless

afterward it yieldeth the peaceable fruit of righteousness unto them which are exercised thereby.
Hebrews 12:11

I Have Years:

For by me thy days shall be multiplied, and the years of thy life shall be increased.
Proverbs 9:11

Z

I Have Zeal:

For I know the forwardness of your mind, for which I boast of you to them of Macedonia, that Achaia was ready a year ago; and your zeal hath provoked very many.
2 Corinthians 9:2

IN CHRIST

There is therefore now no condemnation to them which are in Christ Jesus, who walk not after the flesh, but after the Spirit.
Romans 8:1

For the law of the Spirit of life in Christ Jesus hath made me free from the law of sin and death.
Romans 8:2

Nor height, nor depth, nor any other creature, shall be able to separate us from the love of God, which is in Christ Jesus our Lord.
Romans 8:39

So we, being many, are one body in Christ, and every one members one of another.
Romans 12:5

Unto the church of God which is at Corinth, to them that are sanctified in Christ Jesus, called to be saints, with all that in every place call upon the name of Jesus Christ our Lord, both their's and our's:
1 Corinthians 1:2

But of him are ye in Christ Jesus, who of God is made unto us wisdom, and righteousness, and sanctification, and

redemption:
1 Corinthians 1:30

If in this life only we have hope in Christ, we are of all men most miserable.
1 Corinthians 15:19

Now he which stablisheth us with you in Christ, and hath anointed us, is God;
2 Corinthians 1:21

Now thanks be unto God, which always causeth us to triumph in Christ, and maketh manifest the savour of his knowledge by us in every place.
2 Corinthians 2:14

Therefore if any man be in Christ, he is a new

creature: old things are passed away; behold, all things are become new.
2 Corinthians 5:17

To wit, that God was in Christ, reconciling the world unto himself, not imputing their trespasses unto them; and hath committed unto us the word of reconciliation.
2 Corinthians 5:19

And that because of false brethren unawares brought in, who came in privily to spy out our liberty which we have in Christ Jesus, that they might bring us into bondage:
Galatians 2:4

For ye are all the children of God by faith in Christ Jesus.
Galatians 3:26

There is neither Jew nor Greek, there is neither bond nor free, there is neither male nor female: for ye are all one in Christ Jesus.
Galatians 3:28

For in Christ Jesus neither circumcision availeth any thing, nor uncircumcision, but a new creature.
Galatians 6:15

Paul, an apostle of Jesus Christ by the will of God, to the saints which are at Ephesus, and to the faithful in Christ Jesus:
Ephesians 1:1

Blessed be the God and Father of our Lord Jesus Christ, who hath blessed us with all spiritual blessings in heavenly places in Christ:
Ephesians 1:3

That we should be to the praise of his glory, who first trusted in Christ.
Ephesians 1:12

And hath raised us up together, and made us sit together in heavenly places in Christ Jesus:
Ephesians 2:6

For we are his workmanship, created in Christ Jesus unto good works, which God hath

before ordained that we should
walk in them.
Ephesians 2:10

That the Gentiles should be
fellowheirs, and of the same
body, and partakers of his
promise in Christ by the gospel:
Ephesians 3:6

Paul and Timotheus, the
servants of Jesus Christ, to all
the saints in Christ Jesus which
are at Philippi, with the bishops
and deacons:
Philippians 1:1

Let this mind be in you, which
was also in Christ Jesus:
Philippians 2:5

For we are the circumcision, which worship God in the spirit, and rejoice in Christ Jesus, and have no confidence in the flesh. Philippians 3:3

To the saints and faithful brethren in Christ which are at Colosse: Grace be unto you, and peace, from God our Father and the Lord Jesus Christ. Colossians 1:2

Since we heard of your faith in Christ Jesus, and of the love which ye have to all the saints, Colossians 1:4

In every thing give thanks: for this is the will of God in Christ

Jesus concerning you.
1 Thessalonians 5:18

Paul, an apostle of Jesus Christ by the will of God, according to the promise of life which is in Christ Jesus, 2 Timothy 1:1

Who hath saved us, and called us with an holy calling, not according to our works, but according to his own purpose and grace, which was given us in Christ Jesus before the world began, 2 Timothy 1:9

Hold fast the form of sound words, which thou hast heard of me, in faith and love which is in Christ Jesus.
2 Timothy 1:13

Thou therefore, my son, be
strong in the grace that is in
Christ Jesus.
2 Timothy 2:1

Therefore I endure all things for
the elect's sakes, that they may
also obtain the salvation which
is in Christ Jesus with eternal
glory.
2 Timothy 2:10

Yea, and all that will live godly
in Christ Jesus shall suffer
persecution.
2 Timothy 3:12

And that from a child thou hast
known the holy scriptures,
which are able to make thee wise
unto salvation through faith

which is in Christ Jesus.
2 Timothy 3:15

That the communication of thy
faith may become effectual by
the acknowledging of every good
thing which is in you in Christ
Jesus. Philemon 1:6

Having a good conscience; that,
whereas they speak evil of you,
as of evildoers, they may be
ashamed that falsely accuse your
good conversation in Christ.
1 Peter 3:16

For if these things be in you, and
abound, they make you that ye
shall neither be barren nor
unfruitful in the knowledge of

our Lord Jesus Christ.
2 Peter 1:8

Jude, the servant of Jesus
Christ, and brother of James, to
them that are sanctified by God
the Father, and preserved in
Jesus Christ, and called:
Jude 1

IN HIM

For in him we live, and move, and have our being; as certain also of your own poets have said, For we are also his offspring.
Acts 17:28

For all the promises of God in him are yea, and in him Amen, unto the glory of God by us.
2 Corinthians 1:20

For he hath made him to be sin for us, who knew no sin; that we might be made the righteousness of God in him.
2 Corinthians 5:21

For though he was crucified through weakness, yet he liveth by the power of God. For we

also are weak in him, but we shall live with him by the power of God toward you.
2 Corinthians 13:4

According as he hath chosen us in him before the foundation of the world, that we should be holy and without blame before him in love:
Ephesians 1:4

Having made known unto us the mystery of his will, according to his good pleasure which he hath purposed in himself:
Ephesians 1:9

That in the dispensation of the fulness of times he might gather together in one all things in

Christ, both which are in heaven, and which are on earth; even in him:
Ephesians 1:10

Having abolished in his flesh the enmity, even the law of commandments contained in ordinances; for to make in himself of twain one new man, so making peace;
Ephesians 2:15

And be found in him, not having mine own righteousness, which is of the law, but that which is through the faith of Christ, the righteousness which is of God by faith:
Philippians 3:9

For it pleased the Father that in him should all fulness dwell;
Colossians 1:19

As ye have therefore received Christ Jesus the Lord, so walk ye in him:
Colossians 2:6

Rooted and built up in him, and stablished in the faith, as ye have been taught, abounding therein with thanksgiving.
Colossians 2:7

For in him dwelleth all the fulness of the Godhead bodily.
Colossians 2:9

And ye are complete in him, which is the head of all

principality and power:
Colossians 2:10

That the name of our Lord
Jesus Christ may be glorified in
you, and ye in him, according to
the grace of our God and the
Lord Jesus Christ.
2 Thessalonians 1:12

Who gave himself for us, that he
might redeem us from all
iniquity, and purify unto himself
a peculiar people, zealous of
good works,
Titus 2:14

This then is the message which
we have heard of him, and
declare unto you, that God is
light, and in him is no darkness

at all.
1 John 1:5

He that saith he abideth in him ought himself also so walk, even as he walked.
1 John 2:6

Again, a new commandment I write unto you, which thing is true in him and in you: because the darkness is past, and the true light now shineth.
1 John 2:8

But the anointing which ye have received of him abideth in you, and ye need not that any man teach you: but as the same anointing teacheth you of all things, and is truth, and is no lie,

and even as it hath taught you,
ye shall abide in him.
1 John 2:27

And now, little children,
abide in him; that, when he shall
appear, we may have
confidence, and not be ashamed
before him at his coming.
1 John 2:28

And ye know that he was
manifested to take away our
sins; and in him is no sin.
1 John 3:5

Whosoever abideth in him
sinneth not: whosoever sinneth
hath not seen him, neither know
him.
1 John 3:6

And he that keepeth his commandments dwelleth in him, and he in him. And hereby we know that he abideth in us, by the Spirit which he hath given us.
1 John 3:24

Hereby know we that we dwell in him, and he in us, because he hath given us of his Spirit.
1 John 4:13

IN WHOM

How then shall they call on him in whom they have not believed? and how shall they believe in him of whom they have not heard? and how shall they hear without a preacher?
Romans 10:14

Who delivered us from so great a death, and doth deliver: in whom we trust that he will yet deliver us;
Corinthians 1:10

In whom we have redemption through his blood, the forgiveness of sins, according to the riches of his grace;
Ephesians 1:7

In whom also we have obtained an inheritance, being predestinated according to the purpose of him who worketh all things after the counsel of his own will:
Ephesians 1:11

In whom ye also trusted, after that ye heard the word of truth, the gospel of your salvation: in whom also after that ye believed, ye were sealed with that holy Spirit of promise,
Ephesians 1:13

In whom all the building fitly framed together groweth unto an holy temple in the Lord:
Ephesians 2:21

In whom ye also are builded together for an habitation of God through the Spirit.
Ephesians 2:22

In whom we have boldness and access with confidence by the faith of him.
Ephesians 3:12

In whom we have redemption through his blood, even the forgiveness of sins:
Colossians 1:14

In whom are hid all the treasures of wisdom and knowledge.
Colossians 2:3

In whom also ye are circumcised with the circumcision made

without hands, in putting off the
body of the sins of the flesh by
the circumcision of Christ:
Colossians 2:11

SOIL Foundation, Inc.

All Books can be Purchase from amazon.com, Amazon.co.uk, Amazon.de, Amazon.fr, Amazon.it, Amazon.es, Barnesandnoble.com, ebay.com, (search: Ovbije)

Publication Books

All Day God

Praying the Word From the Book of Timothy

Praying the Word From the Book of Ephesians

Resurrection from the Flood

Coaching to Completion

Praying the Word From the Epistle of John

God Loves Me

God Is With Me
I Am Not Afraid

Praying the Word From the Book of Galatians

Praying the Word From the Book of James

Praying the Word From the Book of Philippians

To God Alone
Praise, Worship & Thanksgivings

Praying the Word From the Book of Colossians

Praying the Word From the Book of Titus

Praying the Word From First Peter

Praying the Word From Psalm 119

Praying the Word From Second Peter

I Am

I Have

Libros en Español

Orando la Palabra
Desde el Libro de Efesios

Dios Me Ama

Tracts:

5 Things God wants you to know

Love Yourself

SONG

Jesus is a friend that will never turn you down

He will never leave you nor forsake you

Call on his name for he is there for you

He will save and guide you to the end

He will save and guide you

REPEAT

By

L. O. Ovbije

www.ingramcontent.com/pod-product-compliance
Lightning Source LLC
Chambersburg PA
CBHW071833020426
42331CB00007B/1707